I, AMDRAIVI

Hannah Maxwell

I, AmDram

OBERON BOOKS
LONDON

WWW.OBERONBOOKS.COM

First published in 2019 by Oberon Books Ltd
521 Caledonian Road, London N7 9RH
Tel: +44 (0) 20 7607 3637 / Fax: +44 (0) 20 7607 3629
e-mail: info@oberonbooks.com
www.oberonbooks.com

PB ISBN: 9781786827463
E ISBN: 9781786827401

Cover image by Daisy King

Printed and bound by 4EDGE Limited, Hockley, Essex, UK.
eBook conversion by Lapiz Digital Services, India.

10 9 8 7 6 5 4 3 2 1

Contents

Foreword

I wrote an article for *The Guardian* a dozen years ago, about amateur dramatics. It was prompted by a new production by the theatre company Proteus, which brought together amdram and professional artists on a new play about Gilbert and Sullivan. Having visited its rehearsals and spoken to the artists, I wrote a piece about amdram's enduring popularity ('Is this,' ran the headline, 'our real national theatre?'), the condescension with which it's often regarded – and the lessons it might teach us about art, creativity and pleasure versus professional obligation.

Had I ever doubted the romance of amdram, that journalistic assignment put me right – not least because (as it happens) it introduced me to my partner and the mother of my children, who was working that day as Proteus's press officer. Some enchanted evening, indeed.

That was the background to my first encounter with Hannah Maxwell's *I, AmDram*, a decade later. She pitched the idea to me in my role as artistic director of Camden People's Theatre, a venue that exists to stage and support work by early-career artists making innovative performance. I had a soft spot for amdram, and was interested in the schism that separates it from professional, high-culture-approved performance. Then along came Hannah – one of those rare artists with a foot in both camps, and (almost) without fear or favour to either – promising a show that would bring amdram, in all its crummy glory, to the CPT stage.

Hannah went on to develop *I, AmDram* on our annual Starting Blocks scheme, which supports solo artists and small companies to make new theatre. It was clear early on that this was a special project with a distinctively wide appeal. An autobiographical coming-out story soundtracked by Rodgers and Hammerstein? An anatomy of one woman's love/hate relationship with home – with tunes by Lerner and Loewe? A Live Artist, tap dancing?

This, surely, was the show to bridge age-old divides and bring audiences of all stripes stampeding to CPT.

But even those high expectations were exceeded by the show Hannah created – the text for which you now hold in your eager hands. Truly, Hannah forded every stream and followed every rainbow to get *I, AmDram* right. The show – first presented at CPT in May 2018 – is beautifully judged, and perfectly balanced. It's contemporary performance *and* it's musical theatre. It dramatises Hannah's own rites-of-passage trajectory (her political, sexual and artistic awakening; her migration to London) without ever self-dramatising. It honours the painful experience of alienation from one's family and home – but does so with grace, good humour and a featherlight touch.

And it refuses to condescend to amdram. Yes, it takes the mickey: it's a very funny show, even more so onstage – where Hannah's brisk self-satirising humour really comes to life – than on the page. Yes, it vividly depicts the crazed jollity of life in a family whose every generation expresses itself largely in Broadway song. And no, it doesn't give a free pass to the casual racism and cultural conservatism with which amdram is often associated.

But finally, this is a celebration of a world – a thriving subculture, let's remember – where performance is a part of everyday life. While the theatre industry worries about how to engage 'normal people' with 'art', the Welwyn Thalians get on with it. And keep on with it, generation after generation, sprinkling a little stardust – and adrenaline, and camaraderie – into the lives of the plumbers, HR managers and sales assistants (as Hannah classifies them) who strut and fret upon their stages.

Is this activity fit to be mentioned in the same breath as the 'wonderfully odd' art that Hannah engages with (and makes) in London? At the very least, they can sit side by side in *I, AmDram*, each equally vital, each fair game for Hannah's sharp wit, each nourishing to her character in their different ways. I see no shadow of a judgment; far from it, the show is an act of love. And a provocation, to audiences from either side of

2

the pro v. amdram divide. To performance-art refuseniks from Hertfordshire as much as to the capital's cultural cognoscenti (apt to be dragooned, as I was, into the Busby Berkeley heroics that bring the show to a close), the question is posed without prejudice: why wouldn't you enjoy *this* as well?

Brian Logan, 2019

Overture

I wanted to write a short introduction to this playtext, to offer a bit more insight into the 'noises off' of the process of writing it and my reasons for wanting (or having) to make a performance about amdram. And to further demonstrate the fathomless depths of my musical theatre knowledge. Then I remembered that I already had the opportunity to write such a piece, two weeks before *I, AmDram* first appeared at CPT. It's even been proofed and edited by some people at *The Guardian*, so it must be safe to repackage here. I hope it does the job.

Some enchanted evenings: my part in
Welwyn Garden City's amdram dynasty

'How do you measure a year in the life?' asks the closing number of Jonathan Larson's *Rent*. It's one of several musicals I know word for word – and one of several my mother is 'not too sure of.' And I know the answer to its question: you can measure the years of my life in musicals. I held my first (and thus far, only) boyfriend's hand through *Little Shop of Horrors*. I came out as queer halfway through rehearsals for *My Fair Lady*. My birth was announced on the opening night of *The King and I*.

I didn't choose this life; I was born into it. My family has been part of the amateur theatre scene in Welwyn Garden City, Hertfordshire, since 1929. That's four generations. My dad's side of the family staged plays at the Barn theatre, my mum's side put on musicals with the Welwyn Thalians Musical and Dramatic Society. Each year of their lives and mine has been mapped by the tensions and tribulations of mounting two or three productions, usually from the classic canon of Gilbert and Sullivan, Rodgers and Hammerstein and a regular churning out of *Oliver!* during 'harder days / Empty larder days.' (Sorry. I can't stop myself.)

Though my experience of amdram was unusually immersive, it's a world known and loved by many across the UK. There are more than 2,500 member societies of the National Operatic and Drama Association, and many more guerrilla operations. My research suggests that on any enchanted evening you are no more than one hundred feet from an open audition for *South Pacific*. In the case of Welwyn's Thalians, nine decades have seen a predictable diminishing from an almost unbelievable heyday. When my great-grandmother was at the directorial helm in the 1930s, shows would pack out with half the population of the embryonic new town. Casts were large, runs were long, the line between amateur and professional was much murkier (Oscar nominee – and later Dame – Flora Robson was an early and active Thalians supporter.) An additional late train (the 10.52pm) was scheduled to take audiences back from Welwyn to London.

I followed in Gran's tap shoes from the ages of seven (as a member of *The Wizard of Oz's* Lullaby League) to eighteen (Harmonising Servant #4 in *My Fair Lady*). Partly for the love of it, partly because it was cheaper for my family to cast me and my brother than to find a babysitter on rehearsal nights. We swelled the ranks of plumbers from Luton, sales assistants from Stevenage and most of Hertfordshire constabulary as cowboys and can-can dancers, with wobbly eyeliner and suspect accents. Membership was predominantly white and middle class, like most of home counties suburbia, yet the feel was and is inclusive. Anyone who walks through the door is welcome to join – amdram needs the bodies for the chorus numbers, you see, as long as they can hold a tune. And even that rule is regularly waived.

It is difficult to paint it three-dimensionally when explaining it to other people, but, for me and my family, the Thalians was so much more than a hobby. It was a secret language, it was a palace we played in, it was a vast library of librettos and anecdotes and local names that we knew intimately. We were privy to the inner sanctums of this world – the gossip, the committee decisions (my grandfather being chairman). We could read the cast list on the kitchen table, its ink still wet, while my mother rang round with the good news and the difficult conversations. Our wardrobes were half-requisitioned for costume storage, our car journeys earmarked for harmonious pre-rehearsal rehearsal.

Alas, the dynasty was sundered by my moving to London for uni and starting a career in queer performance and live art. My lifestyle and politics now tend to jar with the conservative values of amdram. I wince at the same lines I once sang (other than 'A Woman's Touch' from *Calamity Jane*, which elicits a knowing snort of laughter).

I keep the two sides of myself in contact, however, which has made for some interesting crossover episodes. I bring my mother to a lot of live art made by friends and collaborators (she has asked several award-winning artists how on earth they learned all those lines). In turn, I brought the acclaimed lesbian performance-maker and Guggenheim fellow Lois Weaver to my mum's *Guys and Dolls*.

I spent most of my early 20s revelling in my liberal bubble. But recently I've developed more ambivalent feelings about my identity as a small-town exile. If you have left a place – a hometown, a lifestyle, a community theatre group – it is tempting to dismiss everything of that time as an irrelevant preamble to the main event, when you step on stage as the person you want to be viewed as. Perhaps, though, it is worth a return visit: to reconcile those versions of yourself and find what might be worth holding on to, salvaging or celebrating.

Where am I left standing? A progressive, gender-queer performance-maker with a penchant for conservative musical theatre? Or a Thalian on sabbatical, waiting to make my grand return when the amateur rights are released for *Fun Home*? I'm still working that out – and I am, of course, doing a show about it. My mother, meanwhile, is doing *Made in Dagenham*.

Hannah Maxwell

Published in *The Guardian* Online,
Wed 18th April 2018

Written and performed by	Hannah Maxwell
Dramaturgical support	Nick Cassenbaum
	Michelle Madsen
Technical design	Ben Hudson
Production assistance	Livvy Lynch
Recorded voices	Clive Dancey
	Katherine Foxworthy
	Stevie Gibbs
	Alison Gibbs
	Tim Spink
	Amanda Sayers

Developed through the Starting Blocks artist development programme at Camden People's Theatre in 2017 and first performed there on 1st May 2018.

Redeveloped for premiere at the Edinburgh Festival Fringe 2019 with the Pleasance.

With thanks to the eyes of Lucy Bond, Rachel Gammon, Alice Roots and Jen Smethurst, the generosity of Ruth Turner, the casual genius of Daisy King, the pep talks of Tracy Gentles, the timely nudges of Becca Fuller, the tap-dancing talents of Tammy Wall and the *in vino veritas* of Jenny Hunt and Lois Weaver. And to Brian Logan, for everything else.

Special thanks to Serena Grasso at Oberon for somehow making *this* happen.

I, AMDRAM

The audience enter. They all receive a programme, laid out in various fonts and colours. Upon opening, the lyrics to 'It's A Long Way To Tipperary' and 'Pack Up Your Troubles' can be read, upside-down, suggesting a slight issue at the printers.

There is the sound of a small orchestra tuning up. They're not bad.

HANNAH is already on stage, pretty much ready, pottering about. Nervously excited. She might nod at people as they come in. She might wave at people she knows in the audience, and will definitely wave at people she doesn't. Most of the audience will be in no position to tell whether she knows anyone or not. They will look at their grinning friends a few rows forward, as HANNAH mimes at them the question 'You staying for a drink after?' and wonder why Keith and Julie didn't mention that they were friends with the Artist when they all bought the tickets.

On stage can be seen the following, in various corners: a black tailcoat, with a red flower in the button-hole, over a blue waistcoat; a straw boater fringed with green ribbon; a grey tailcoat with a matching top hat; a green suitcase with a green book leant against it; a small blond wig; a pair of black 'character' tap shoes, and two chairs together, centre stage, facing forward. As mentioned, there is also HANNAH, wearing black, backstage-y T-shirt and trousers.

Hanging above in the upstage-right corner is a small TV/monitor. The screen is blue.

Note: if there is the option to have some fancy velvet curtains (red ones, ideally) closed at the front of the stage, they will absolutely be utilised. In which case none of the above will be visible, but HANNAH will still most likely be peeking and waving in the aforementioned manner.

The doors are closed. The houselights remain on. HANNAH puts on the waistcoat, not particularly quickly. She smiles at the audience.

HANNAH: Hi everyone. I'm not sure how to start this.

She picks up the boater and turns it over in her hands.

So if it's okay with you, I'm just going to borrow an idea that I know has worked quite well in the past. Lots of times.

She puts on the boater.

TV switches to a fuzzy recording of the Welwyn Thalians' 'Old Time Music Hall' in 2009. The song 'Let's All Go To The Music Hall' by Harry Claff is being played on piano. Six people stride onto a small stage, fringed with red curtains, wearing boaters and blue and white striped blouses/waistcoats. They include HANNAH's mum and stepdad. HANNAH faces the TV and absentmindedly mirrors the dance moves, singing along under her breath.

As the song ends, and a man in a tailcoat begins to enter the frame, the TV goes blank. HANNAH drops the boater upside down on the floor in a downstage corner. She takes a moment to carefully put on the tailcoat, facing upstage.

She turns around and claps her hands. The lights snap to a sharp, centre spot on her, emcee-style. In the light, the little Union Jacks emblazoning the blue waistcoat can be seen.

HANNAH: *(Channelling her grandfather.)* GOOD evening ladies and gentlemen.

How are we, are we well?

Excellent marvellous fabulous.

HELLO and welcome to another year of this old rubbish.

I'm sure there's no other way you would rather spend your Friday evening than right here with us!

(Peering into audience.) Now where have we come from tonight…

Do we have anyone in from Hitchin?

No? No, I would have thought this was far too low-brow for them.

Anyone in from Stevenage?

Well, yes this is far too high-brow for them!

Anyone from further afield?

(Audience member shouts out or HANNAH picks someone.)

Where? Good lord, and you've come all the way for
this nonsense,
Fancy that. Well, you have excellent taste, Sir –
er, Madam.

NOW. Ladies and Gentlemen,
we have a delightful array of musical and dramatic
delectation for you tonight;
I will be your Chairman for this evening,
banging my gavel in my little perch over there.
We have our musical maestro, tickling the ivories over
there, Mr Peter Farrell! *(Gestures towards keyboard.)*
And our technical department, keeping it well within
the family,
we have our spotlight operator at the back *(Gestures at spot.)*
my grandson, Master Jonathan – I mean, William Maxwell!
Just behind the curtain here *(Gestures SR.)* we have
Madame Director, my lovely wife,
And behind this curtain here *(Gestures SL.)* we have our
Stage Manager Hannah, my granddaughter,
offstage for once, as she's doing her O-Levels!
Not O-Levels now, what are they? GCBs.

AND as always we have a giggling gaggle of lovely
young ladies
at the bar waiting to bring you your fish and chips in
the interval.
If you require a *bever-rarrrge* before then,
then please raise you hand *(Raising hand.)*
raise it high in the air, and they will come a-rushing over
to attend to your tiniest whim,

(To someone in front row.)

...no matter how tiny your whim may be, Sir.

RIGHT, we better get on with it or we'll be here all night!
Before I introduce you to your first act for this evening,
we will start how we always do…by making you do all the work!
No groans, no moans, you knew what you signed up for!

(Houselights come up higher.)

SO, you'll find your song-sheets on your tables,
next to the *mayonaisses* –
Open them up and you'll find a couple of the oldest of
old favourites.
If you remember them, sing them loud and proud.
If like me you've forgotten everything, then sing them
louder and prouder!
We'll begin with that famous number,
'It's A Long Way to Essingdon'!
One and two –

The audience sing 'It's A Long Way to Tipperary' from their programmes. HANNAH sings boomingly along as her grandfather, keeping time with a lot of unnecessary arm swinging. Quieter members of the audience are given additional arm-swinging encouragement, or have an ear cupped at them and an eyebrow raised.

HANNAH: Excellent marvellous fabulous -
    you're the best Friday night audience we've had all week!
    Moving swiftly on, off we go with 'Pack Up Your Troubles'!
    One and two and –

The audience sing 'Pack Up Your Troubles'.

HANNAH: WELL DONE, well done indeed.
    BUT, we shall not be stopping there.
    Ladies and gentlemen, girls and boys
    we will once again be attempting the impossible…

(Gesturing at one side of the audience.)

14

Everyone on this side, all the good-looking people,
will be singing 'It's A Long Way To Tipperary'…

(Gesturing at the other side.)

And everyone on this side, all the intelligent people,
will be singing 'Pack Up Your Troubles'…
At the same time, without the aid of a safety net,
and remember,
(As herself.) If I stop, you keep going.
And it starts 'It's a– / Pack', okay?
'It's a– / Pack'.
… See you on the other side.
One and two, 'It's a– / Pack' –

*Both songs are sung together. HANNAH dips in and out of helping
either side as required.*

*As the last 'Pack up / It's a long way' line begins, HANNAH leaves
the spotlight and it fades.*

The lights come down. Upstage is softly lit in blue.

Footage of the Welwyn Thalians' 2003 production of The Wizard
of Oz *can be seen dimly on the TV: two dozen munchkins crawl
out from behind plasterboard flower-bushes to 'meet the young lady
who fell from a star.'*

*A recording of CLIVE's voice plays, in which other people and activity
can be heard in the background.*

CLIVE: I don't actually know, because every time you…
You're on the side of the stage about to go on a show,
you go, 'Why do I do this? Why do I–?' You're so scared,
adrenaline's going. But once you get on stage, y'know,
y'just – I don't know, y'just…just go with it.

*The TV goes blank. HANNAH, in black backstage-y gear, picks up
the green suitcase and book and walks centre stage as the lights come*

back, cold, with a square shining on the floor from the SL wing.
She places the case in front of the SR chair, the book on top of it,
and sits in the SL one.

HANNAH: I'm sat down on a train.

I'm on my own.

Obviously.

I take this service a handful of times every year, and it's always the same.

I sit by the window *(Look out SR.)*

with my back to where I'm coming from.

I bring a book

kick back

put my feet up on the seat opposite.

I'm not doing that now though,

as, for the purposes of *your* sightlines *(Indicates person sat in front.)*

I haven't put a chair in front of me.

I have put one next to me though.

Otherwise how could you be expected to believe that I'm on a train?

You see, in shows,

two chairs together, centre stage, facing forward,

usually signifies some kind of transport.

The protagonist is there,

they've got a little suitcase

we're on our way somewhere.

There's nothing in the suitcase, by the way –

(Lifting case.) It's just a prop to indicate travel.

It doesn't have to be a train:

could be a car, *(Mimes steering wheel.)*

or a horse and buggy – *(Mimes holding reigns.)*

(In US accent.) 'A little surry with the fringe on top –'

depending, of course, on hand position –
but in this instance, it *is* a train
A particular one.

On the TV, a crawler appears:

'This is a First Capital Connect service to Welwyn Garden City, calling at Finsbury Park, Potters Bar, Hatfield and Welwyn Garden City. The next station is Finsbury Park.'

It's a First Capital Connect service
from King's Cross St Pancras
to Welwyn Garden City
W. G. C.
in Hertfordshire.
It takes about twenty-five minutes and stops at
Finsbury Park
Potters Bar
Hatfield
and Welwyn

The train hasn't left the station yet.
Obviously.
You'll be able to tell when it does
because the movement of the train
will begin to move my body around like this:
(Bounces about in chair a bit, and continues.)
Not just me; everyone and everything else on the train
will continue to be bounced about like this
until we pull into the next station,
or encounter a leaf,
or I try and remember my lines
and forget to keep doing this…
(Still bobbling about.)
The train's left now.

There are two groups of reasons I take this train:
family occasions – birthdays, Christmas, etcetera –
(Gestures on one hand.)
and musical theatre. *(Gestures with other hand, which turns
into 'jazz hands'.)*
There's a lot of crossover between the two.
When I was growing up,
we took the same train for the same reasons
but in the opposite direction.
I was taken to a West End musical for five of my seven
teenage birthdays;
three of those times it was *Les Mis.*

We couldn't see professional shows in Welwyn,
as explained in *Welwyn Garden City Past*
(Presents the cover of the book.)
The author describes it thusly in his overture.

(In RP voice.) 'As far as culture be concerned, the town
is ARID, boasting not one museum, art gallery or
professional theatre.'

(Slams book shut.) So that's where we're going.

I'm feeling vaguely…something something…
so I put down the book
and look out the window *(Looks out SL.)* which, as the
more astute of you will recall,
I earlier mimed as being over there *(Gesture SR.)*

*(The light coming from SR snaps off and is replaced by light
from SL.)*

We begin to ease through a handful of tunnels
and graffitied canyons of brick,
and little by little
the city falls away

into fields and parks and golf courses –
ironically very green and very damp for somewhere
so ARID –
and, as the smoky town dissipates,
the familiar slight anxiety
starts to quietly rumble…
but I'm on my way now.
The doors are closed.
I'm making my prodigal's pilgrimage once again.
Do try to 'get on board.'

The TV shows a crawler:

'This station is Finsbury Park.'

The synthetic train announcement voice plays:

VOICE: This station is… Finsbury Park.

A 'sting' of music plays, like the final 'ta-da!' chords of an upbeat chorus number in Chicago *or* Guys and Dolls, *perhaps. During this, HANNAH jumps up, spins about, and lands on one knee facing the audience with her arms wide, jazz hands a-buzz and a full tits-and-teeth grin. The music ends and she is breathing heavily, possibly off-balance, possibly having hurt her knee.*

HANNAH: That just means that that bit's over now.

HANNAH pushes one of the chairs forward and lifts the case onto it, spinning it around. The other side reveals the titles of several musicals, cut and pasted from old Thalians posters. The TV begins to show a series of old images from the Thalians archive, of various family members in various productions.

The Welwyn THALIANS Musical and Dramatic Society
was established in Welwyn Garden in nineteen-
TWENTY-nine.
Founding members included my grandmother's mother

and my grandfather's father.
They put on two musical productions every year,
in the spring and autumn:
one 'Old Time Music Hall',
and one *oldey timey* musi*cal.*
Things like *South Pacific, Oklahoma!, (Not So) Thoroughly
Modern Millie…*
In eighty-nine years, that's some 178 different shows,
each of which has involved at least two of my relatives,
often closer to seven – including my mum *(Looks to blond wig.)*
my stepdad *(To boater.)*
grandad *(To tailcoat.)*
nan *(To tap shoes.)*
and gran. *(Taps the suitcase.)*
I am the first female member of my family to miss being
in a Thalians show for a reason other than pregnancy.

It wasn't just my family in these shows –
we're not a cult…technically –
we just swelled the ranks
of plumbers from Luton,
HR managers from St Albans,
sales assistants from Stevenage;
a motley crew ready to give up
their evenings and weekends to dress up
as cowboys and debutantes
and gangsters and prostitutes
and prance around
and sing in eight-part harmony
at the double or triple weddings that most old musicals
end happily with.

We're talking Rodgers and Hammerstein,
Gilbert and Sullivan,

Lerner and Loewe –
you may not have heard of them,
but you'll definitely have *heard* them.

We're talking spit 'n' sawdust,
we're talking tits 'n' teeth,
we're designing posters which push WordArt to its
very limits.
We're keeping the waistbands wide,
the hearts big
and the racism casual.

It's difficult to get across quite how much of a big deal
this is in my family.
Maybe you don't really get musicals.
Maybe they're not really your kind of 'Art'.
Maybe you find their dated depictions of normative
gender roles and white privilege problematic,
and I hear where you're coming from.

This is where I'm coming from.

If you've ever seen the film *The Godfather*,
you know that one slightly more reluctant son,
who may not have necessarily *liked* organised crime,
may not have had a natural affinity for it...
but family's family.
And sometimes you have to help bury a body.
Or, in my case,
take a week out of uni to stage manage *Oliver!*

Okay, I need to do a set change.
Not a very complicated one, but still,
we're talking about amateur dramatics,
'amdram',

and we're going to do it authentically,
so Livvy? *(Technician's name.)*
Can we have a long and awkward blackout please?

Blackout.

Things are moved about in the darkness, inefficiently. Something might be dropped. HANNAH might bump into something. There is a muffled exclamation of 'Shit!'

Silence.

HANNAH: This is kind of nice, isn't it?
I'm done with the scene change,
but I just thought I'd use this opportunity
to lead us all in a sort of group study session on the nature of the long blackout.
You don't get very many blackouts, long or otherwise, in professional productions these days,
everything's so slickly choreographed.
But still in some amateur productions, you might be sat

in the dark
in silence
for thirty to forty days,
waiting for the lights to come back on and reveal, perhaps a single chair.

Don't get me wrong –
I *love* a long blackout.
I don't think we should be pandering to my generation's shortening attention spans.
And theatre involves living people;
maybe it should be truer to life than the quick cutaways and snappy edits of film and television.
For life, as we know, contains moments of pause…
downtime…

22

space for reflection…
waiting for buses to come
and kettles to boil…
and these moments of stillness are good for us.
Good for the brain.
Good for the soul.

Pause.

For in our consumer capitalist culture
we expect everything to be handed to us ready-made,
with no thought spared as to where it came from.
Think of the clothes on our backs,
the food in our fridges,
the phones in our hands.
Phones which, incidentally, you cannot sneakily check
if you are bored in a long blackout.
I don't want things to hide their mechanisms.
When the lights come on,
at long last, and reveal that chair,
I want to know exactly where it came from
and exactly what it took to get it there.
I want to have heard things clatter to the floor backstage
in pursuit of that same chair.
I want to appreciate the intricate backstage subplot,
having heard someone hiss from the wings:
'Nigel – where's that fucking chair??'
and Nigel to respond gruffly, from the opposite side
of the stage,
that he does not know where the fucking chair is, it is not
where Judith left it.
I want to see a shadowy figure stride purposefully halfway
across the stage,
with a similar, but yet entirely wrong chair,

before being yanked back behind the curtain and made to
swap it out.
I want to feel in my back teeth
the scrape and screech
of four wooden legs
being dragged into six different arrangements
by two warring backstage factions
in disagreement as to which bit is actually next
and what demands that bit makes upon said chair.
And when finally,
after what feels like an eternity,
the lights come up
and we behold that chair,
we will know it,
we will love it,
already, before it's even done anything.

The lights come up. There is a chair.

The TV shows a crawler:

'This station is Potter's Bar.'

We hear the following announcement from the pleasing female voice:

VOICE: This station is... Potter's Bar.

HANNAH walks offstage.

*(Another) blackout. Soft blue light at the back. The TV plays an
excerpt of the Thalians' 2007 production of* Annie Get Your Gun:
*four awkward, skinny can-can dancers high-kick in front of a dozen
cowboys old enough to be their dads, and indeed some of them are.
The voice of Kat can be heard, with other voices in the background
(including a loud, cackle-like burst of laughter):*

KAT: 'You get stressed. You get hyped. It's like you're on
drugs a little bit. Waiting in the wings, and you're like

24

dancing like no one's watching – you wouldn't normally do that…like, but it's the adrenaline rush, it's like you've had…a lot of drugs.'

Warm light rushes back. HANNAH re-enters quickly and marches front and centre, sniffing.

HANNAH: This is what it was like:

every Wednesday, when I was growing up,

we would go for dinner at my grandparents' house.

My grandparents will hereafter be referred to as Nan *(Shoes.)* and Poppa. *(Tailcoat.)*

They lived in Welwyn Garden City, quite close to the town centre:

(Eyes closed, miming the route.) you come out the station,

on the good side of town,

the West side (story),

down to the fountain,

take a right,

keep the theatre on your left,

over the white bridge,

and there they are.

My brother and I arrive first after school.

He plonks down square in front of the TV,

one of those old glass ones where you could feel the static on your nose.

I wander off into the Green Room, *(Approaches keyboard.)* what we call the unheated extension at the side of the house.

Light slowly closes onto the keyboard. The TV begins to show a looping video of a flickering wood fire. Now and then, HANNAH plays – (Snippets of familiar tunes.)

It contained a dining table,

an old grandfather clock

and my great-grandmother's old piano.
(Runs hands over it.) It was huge,
heavy, wooden, with a lid that snapped your fingers…
this isn't it.
Arranged on top are faded photographs
and tattered librettos from long-forgotten shows –
such classics as *The Merry Englander*
and *Yeomen Of The Guard.*
There are knickknacks from Poppa's time working at Hatfield
House as Henry Tudor – *(I'm 'Ennery the Eighth I am)*
A bowl of wax fruit –
('ave a banana)
– fake flowers.

HANNAH places a small bunch of plastic flowers on top of the keyboard.

– and several candles.

HANNAH places some plastic candles on top of the keyboard.

These are fake, obviously.
But they are the genuine ones that Nan has in her house.

At quarter past five Mum arrives, flops on the sofa,
and chats with Nan about the trials and tribulations of
whatever show is coming up: *(there's no business like show business)*
We snack on the obscene amount of sugary goods Poppa
will have bought in especially from Morrisons: *(lots of chocolate for me to eat)*
Unless the *Daily Express* have declared a HEAT WAVE,
the fire will be roaring: *(lots of coal making lots of heat)*
Well, not actually a fire. It's actually just a wall-mounted
heater that plays a video of a fireplace. There are five
different settings:

The TV flicks between the following footages as they are mentioned, before returning to log fire:

gas fire, coal fire, log fire, babbling brook and lava lamp.

At quarter to six my stepfather Peter gets in –
(a policeman's lot is not a happy one, (happy one))
and we all sit up at the table and dive in to fish and chips.
Conversation attempts to stick to what's going on at school, or the office,

when the kitchen is going to be done up,

but is incessantly interrupted by my parents and grandparents breaking into song. They can be set off by a single word: *(I don't believe a word of it, a single blinking word of it)*

– I have no idea what that is or where it's from, but I have heard it erupt from them literally hundreds of times.

Harmonies are often involved

As luck would have it, Nan is a soprano: *(High octave flourish.)*

Mum is an alto: *(Middle octave flourish.)*

as am I: *(Middle octave flourish.)*

and so was William: *(Middle octave flourish.)*

until he hit puberty, and dropped to Peter's tenor: *(Low octave flourish.)*

but not quite Poppa's bass: *(Very low octave flourish.)*

Around the food and chatter and musical interludes
breaks my mother's laughter like the shattering of glass:
(Rhythm of loud 'alto' chord, accelerando, like something falling down stairs.)
(HANNAH laughs, channelling her mother.)
(Yelled over the top of music.) Harmonically joined by Nan:
(Addition of high notes to chord.)
AND SOMETIMES EVEN ME...

(Addition of lower notes to chord, which is then allowed to fade.)

…which is *worrying.*

Pause.

Sometimes I don't find things funny.

I fancy myself a particularly complex and brooding teenager.

In these instances, I return to the Green Room for some alone time.

*(Opening instrumental of 'On My Own' from **Les Miserables**.)*

Name it?

A guess from the audience, hopefully correct.

I usually hammer out something plaintive,

in stark counterpoint to the musical merriment still emanating from the kitchen.

Perhaps 'I Giorni' by Ludovico Einaudi,

which was and remains the only song I can play with both hands.

HANNAH begins to play 'I Giorni' emotively, tenderly, with both hands, as the lights close in, becoming fringed with blue. For the most part the words are spoken over the softly held chords, or else in the quiet between each delicate phrase of music; this is because it is very difficult to play piano and deliver lines simultaneously.

(As she plays.) In the spring of 2010, two things were happening…

the Thalians were beginning work on their next big show,

and I was coming to terms with my sexuality.

This period of time nearly tore my family apart,

as dinners devolved into shouting matches,

sides were taken,

no small amount of tears were shed…

My mother and my grandmother

couldn't decide which of them should get to direct
My Fair Lady.

HANNAH stops playing abruptly and the lights return to previous state.

You may laugh *(And they hopefully have.)*
…you have no idea.
Eventually they smoothed things out and agreed to co-direct,
moving the conversation on to who was going to audition
for what role.
Peter was interested in the acerbic misogynist, Professor
Henry Higgins,
Poppa was interested in the affable Colonel Pickering,
and mother was interested in *me* going for Eliza.
Doolittle.
The lead.
I was eighteen, ***(going on nineteen)***
just shy of the twenty years Julie Andrews had
when she debuted as Eliza on Broadway.
And, twenty years ago, Mum had been Eliza…
('I could have danced all night' played in the middle octave.)
and, twenty years before that, Nan…
(The same, played an octave higher.)
and… Gran
(The same, played an octave even higher.)
…but I wasn't sure I could quite *get up there.*

I felt far more comfortable with 'Street Where You Live'
(First bar of 'Street Where You Live'.)
(Sings the first line, somewhat haltingly.)
which is the main song sung by Freddie Eynsford-Hill,
the secondary male tenor,
a dapper young idiot
who falls hopelessly in love with Eliza.

29

I had already been practicing, in the private echo of my parents' garage:

(Second bar of 'Street Where You Live'.)

(Sings the secind line as she plays.)

When I had it down pat I approached my mother
and floated the idea of auditioning for Freddie…
I can't remember exactly how that conversation went.
I don't think she thought I was being serious.
Not entirely sure how serious I was at eighteen.
In any case the idea was swiftly dismissed with one of her
well-meaning, signature cackles:

HANNAH does her mother's laugh, in time with the fast rhythm of the chords. This is gradually joined by the opening chords of Robyn's 'Dancing On My Own' (2010). She leaves the keyboard to centre stage, dragging the chair behind her.

(Standing between the two chairs.)

Two things came out in 2010:
me and this song.

The music cuts to the second verse:

('Gay-ing' up her hair.) I cut and dyed my hair, looking not
unlike Robyn herself.
This meant that if I wanted to audition for Eliza,
I would have to borrow my mother's wiglet.

HANNAH runs to the blonde 'wiglet' and clips it haphazardly to her head. As the song hits the emphatic chorus, HANNAH joins in on the best lines, most of the time as an upper harmony. Alongside this aural treat, HANNAH produces a small bottle of whiskey from somewhere, takes a mouthful, gargles and spits into the corner of the stage. She takes out a nasal inhalator and takes a big huff up each nostril. She dances about a bit. She stretches her neck. She physically and psychologically gears herself up.

She strides between the chairs and the song slides into the instrumental of 'I Could Have Danced All Night' from My Fair Lady.

HANNAH: *(Awkward, femme-ish, less confidently alright at singing than she was a moment ago, she sings the opening lines.)*

(Speaking over the music.) I did go for Eliza in the end,
up on stage in front of the whole society,
with Nan and Mum behind a big desk, *X-Factor* style.
Peter got Higgins –
Poppa got Pickering –
and I might have been fine if it had been in this octave:

(Incorrectly alto, she rejoins the song with a phrase about having no idea what made the dance so exciting.)

But actually it's–
(Correctly, painfully, soprano, she sings the next line.)

(With sincere effort, humiliation swelling behind her eyes, she struggles on through the last lines of the song, explaining how she could absolutely have danced, danced, danced ALL–)

'Fuck it.' The wiglet is wrenched from her scalp and flung to the floor. She turns her back to the audience, leaning on the chairs, exhausted, back-sweat shadowing her shirt. The final chords crescendo around her for what seems an age; an age in which Mum, Nan, Gran and Julie Andrews would have been able to hold that mountainous high 'G' spot.

Quiet. Breathing. HANNAH swivels back around with a look of severe intensity.

HANNAH: And in that moment…
my voice cracked on the high note…
I saw Mum and Nan wince…
the blood rushed to my cheeks
(Indicating fallen wiglet.) …and a century's lineage lay
abash-ed on the floor.

Tammy got it.[1]

HANNAH walks up to the wiglet and casually punts it into the front row, perhaps muttering 'one-nil' to herself as she does so. She exits SL.

Blackout, soft blue upstage. The TV shows footage from the Thalians' Little Shop Of Horrors *(2006), in which a numerous cast in grey and green costumes do some simple choreography around a large and not particularly convincing man-eating plant.*

KAT's voice can be heard, laughter and activity in the background:

KAT: I was talking about your mum yesterday… *(Laughs.)*
…and I was saying that actually, as far as directors go, she's probably the best director that I've had to work with. And I love how animated she is all the time… (they're staring at me!) *(Laughs.)* …yeah, she's SO animated and I love – at the end of rehearsal, when we're all kind of relaxing, how she becomes the performer, and like she'll tell these stories that have happened and she, she uses her hands and everything – I love that about her.

The fuzzy background noises from the recording continue, clarifying. A lot of people in an echoey space. Smatterings of piano being played intermittently. Chuckling. Not-quite-right harmony lines being practised at half-strength. An animated female voice breaking over the melee, chivvying various cohorts into position. A Welwyn Thalians rehearsal.[2]

---

1   Tammy Wall, Thalian leading lady material since 2002. Definitely deserved it. No hard feelings.

2   This should be played at a level to suggest all of this, but not loud enough to identify specific tunes or words. Sound recordings were made not at a *My Fair Lady* rehearsal in 2010, but at a *Made In Dagenham* one in 2018. This revelation would no doubt shatter the theatrical illusion.

HANNAH is at the side of the stage, poised, hands together at breast level. She is holding one of the plastic candles. She walks part-way across the stage, whilst singing:

HANNAH: 'Poor… Professor Higgins.'
    (Yelled, channeling her mother.) No!

She brings her feet together, sort of to attention, and turns front.

Thalians rehearsals take place at Thalian Hall,
on the East Side of town (ooh-er).
(Eyes closed, miming the route.) You come out of the station,
over the barbed wire footbridge,
past the disused Shredded Wheat factory
And there it is… *(Holds up candle.)*
opposite the B&Q.

She puts the candle down on the stage and walks back to the side, picks up another candle and makes the same journey across the stage, getting slightly further, whilst singing:

'Poor… Professor Higgins.'
    (Yells as MUM.) Again!

Feet together, turns front.

I may not have been cut out for Eliza,
but I did get cast…
as Harmonising Servant Number Four, *(Holds up candle.)*
one of seven,
with one shitty song in the second half that mum makes
us do
(Whilst walking round again.) over and over and over and

(Picking up candle, back across stage.)
'Poor… Professor Higgins.'
    (As MUM.) Not quite!

(Turning front, getting flustered.) And all the while
I had to watch the guy they cast as Freddie,
(Looks sourly at candle.) …Tim.
Over twice the age Freddie is supposed to be,
mutilating his song and fucking up the dances.
(Warbling a snatch of 'Street Where You Live', an unfair impression.)

*Walking quickly back round, grabs a candle, with give-a-shit
attitude–*

'Poor… Professor Higgins.'
(MUM's verdict.) What was that!?

(Turns front, huffily.)
Let me be clear: as an advocate for inter-generational
arts practice, there's no reason an older person can't play
Freddie – my issue was not with him, it was more about –
okay, my *issue* was…
(Slams down candle and walks forward, directly at audience.)
…that in this world where every emotion is spontaneously
expressed in song,
where strangers on the street might just start two-stepping
around each other,
where plasterers from Harpenden can be Gentleman of
Japan,
and Baptists from Baldock can be Russian Jews from
Anatefke,
where mothers of four can be virgin maids,
and grizzled pensioners can be teenage heartthrobs,
for some reason all this merry suspension of disbelief
could not be extended
to eighteen-year-old me
and my scarcely two-year-old tits.

To quote Henry Higgins himself:

why CAN'T a woman be more like a man?
(Accusatory eyebrow movement, which implicates the audience in their own preconceptions about gender and their compliance in the enforcement of societal roles along a binary notion of what it means to be 'man' or 'woman'.)

(Realising she has something else to be doing.) – oh shit!

HANNAH rushes back around, picking up the last candle, hurrying to the final point on the opposite side of the stage, where one may imagine six choral singers in servants' attire are waiting, with the third and fifth spaced passive-aggressively apart.

'Poor… Professor Higgins.'
(Maternal fury.) Hannah!!

Mum snips at me for being distracted during rehearsals, which happens a lot this year, what with exam stress, applying to unis,
(With agonised gestures.) Desperate Obsession With Girl Down My Street –
but that's no excuse to not learn your harmony lines.
And she has a lot on her plate as well; there's a cast of thirty, creative differences with my grandmother,
and they've hired a set which is so huge,
(Picturing, indicating.) that when Eliza appears, in her ballgown,
at the top of Higgins's staircase…
you can only see her knees.

(Tweaking the candles' positions.) …and there's only eight months to get it right.

HANNAH poises herself with hands clasped before her. Holding her frame, she weaves between the rows of candles.

'Poor… Professor Higgins
Poor… Professor Higgins

On she plods, against all odds
Oh, poor… Amanda Sayers!'

(With the static, chaste choreography of the Servants' Chorus.)

'Monday nights, Thursday nights
8pm to 10pm
Year on in, year on out
Ninety fucking years!'

Blackout.

The TV shows a crawler.

'This station is Hatfield.'

We hear the following announcement from the pleasing female voice:

VOICE: This station is… Hatfield.

The TV switches to an excerpt from the Thalians' 2008 production of South Pacific*; girls and women of various ages dance in swimwear, with towels, before a painted beachfront backdrop, clearly keen to wash the patriarchy right outta their hair.*

STEVIE's voice can be heard:

STEVIE: *South Pacific (HANNAH's voice: 'Calamity Jane?'), South Pacific* and *Calamity Jane.* Hannah and I were fantastic dancers. *(Laughing.)* Fantastic can-canners! *(HANNAH's voice: 'We were the lead dancers!')* Of course. *(HANNAH's voice: 'The Welwyn Thalians, we were the lead dancers.')* And our beautiful dressing room that our mothers moaned about every night, of how horribly messy it was.

The TV shows a crawler:

'This station is Welwyn Garden City.'

We hear the following announcement from the pleasing female voice:

VOICE: This station is… Welwyn Garden City.

The lights return, and reveal a sizeable backdrop, painted to look like the town centre of Welwyn Garden City. Red brick, green lawns, grey pavements. Trees. A fountain. HANNAH stands looking at it, quietly. She picks up the suitcase. She steps out as Doris Day begins to sing 'Just Blew In From The Windy City' from Calamity Jane.

HANNAH walks forward and puts down the case. She looks around slowly, unimpressed. The muscles are tense around her eyes, hands are thrust in her pockets. She chews her cheeks some. She produces a tube of filter tips out of her back pocket. She takes one out and perches it between her lips. She takes out a pouch of rolling tobacco, continuing to look around, sour and louche. She struggles to get the pouch open and ends up ripping it. Tobacco goes everywhere. She performs a short 'urgh, what a fucking day' bit for the strangers she assumes are watching her. She shakes the baccy off of herself, and tries to brush it away with her feet, as Doris can be heard announcing that 'the dance that they did there…went something like this —'

HANNAH finds her feet skidding and shuffling the tobacco around in some sort of rhythm. She is perturbed. They start clicking in a manner that veers dangerously close to tap dancing. She still has a filter tip between her lips. She skips around in a sort of circle, still looking confused. She starts to get on board with the idea and undertakes some definite 'moves', jumping to the side and back, kicking out, dragging her toe in a wide ring to make a noise consistent with the sound of Doris's iconic sapphic cowboy boots scraping on spilt salt.[3]

The music picks up, and urges HANNAH on to ever greater choreographic feats: some complicated leaping over the suitcase, lurching back and forth, jumping and clicking her heels, before the rhythm finally slows and allows her to gently step-together, step-behind for two more bars, pick up the suitcase, pose in a silhouetted light, and, on the final beat, spit a filter tip into the audience.

---

3 Tobacco won't make that scraping noise, but crumbled Shredded Wheat will.

Mum and Uncle David in *Sweeney Todd* at the Barn Theatre, c. 1985

Nanny and Poppa in *The Boyfriend*, maybe? c. 1970

A very old Thalians show, involving togas and deckchairs. God knows, c. 1960

The 'Ascot Gavotte' in *My Fair Lady*, c. 1975. Nan in black, second from the left

Contact sheet of (Great) Gran, c. 1975

Poppa as Higgins in *My Fair Lady*, c. 1975

Mum, back row with the big eyes, in the chorus of *The Gondoliers*, c. 1982

Me as a flower girl in *My Fair Lady*, 2010, second from the right (Tammy as Eliza centre)

Nan, in *H.M.S. Pinafore*, probably, c. 1975

Gran receives the Director's bouquet,
Poppa on the right, c. 1985

Mum and Uncle Jon in *The Wizard
of Oz,* c. 1974

Blackout. Rapturous applause fades until only HANNAH's heavy breathing can be heard.

Houselights come up. HANNAH is drinking from a bottle of water.

HANNAH: It's the interval now. Every show needs an interval. You could go for a wee, get a drink. You should be aware though, that in a Thalians show, no one tends to leave during an interval, because the bar is a bit of a walk away and they're all older than god. I'm sure we don't have that problem here tonight. You are all remaining seated because you want to see what I might do next. Blurring the boundaries of performance and real life. Expanding the definition of what constitutes entertainment.

HANNAH asks someone in the audience to sweep up the Shredded Wheat, using a broom just offstage. Meanwhile she undresses, down to her tan tights, boxers and an ill-fitting, frilly off-white bra.

Sorry, this is a bit of an in-joke. Back in the day, when my mum was backstage with the ladies' chorus, getting changed with everybody, she was renowned for revealing these ratty, grey bras that were older than she was. Now, I haven't owned a bra since 2015. But she was kind enough to lend me this one for tonight.

HANNAH asks someone in the front row to pass some wet wipes hidden under their seat. She does a quick pits-and-bits once-over, then chucks it offstage. She gets into trousers, shirt, waistcoat and green tie.

When the sweeper is finished sweeping, she gets them to collect her make-up bag from offstage.

HANNAH: How much longer do we have, Livvy?

LIVVY: (Four minutes!)

HANNAH gets the audience member to apply eyeliner, whilst she chats a bit to them about where they're from, and/or their favourite musical. There are wrong answers. Once done, they are asked to put the bag back and return to their seat.

HANNAH: How long now?

LIVVY: (Two minutes!)

A little bit of waiting.

HANNAH: *(Filling the silence.)* How's it going from your end? I'm having a lot of fun. Just wish there were a couple of scenes I wasn't in!
(To audience member nearest.) Chuck us that wiglet.

She combs out the wiglet with her fingers.

Hard as it may be to believe, I didn't actually carve out a career in musical theatre, unless this counts. (It doesn't.) No, I work primarily as a Creative Collaborator and Project Coordinator in the fields of Experimental Performance and Live Art.

She holds up the wiglet with one hand, like the skull of Yorick.

(Inspecting the wiglet carefully.) I first encountered the field at university. Mum had wanted me to study something more 'academic'.

*The wiglet is animated with the idiosyncratic movement of her mother. HANNAH **'does her voice'** along with the 'puppeteering'; a hyperbolised caricature, somewhere between* Absolutely Fabulous *and Gemma Jones in* Bridget Jones's Diary.

'Why can't you just do drama as a hobby??'

Well, first of all, it's not 'drama', it's Performance Art.

'So…theatre?'

No, it's not theatre, and it's not a hobby, it's…it's *a research engine, driven by artists, who are working across forms, contexts, and spaces to open up new languages for the representation of ideas and identities.* (Thank you to the Live Art Development Agency for that quote!)

'The Whatty McWhat agency?'

Doesn't matter – it's the intellectual and aesthetic freedom to create meaning through image, text, ritual, noise, literally any potentiality brought forth from an observed, *live* human body. *(Gestures down torso – the wiglet follows the gesture with its 'eyes'.)*

'Oh dear, you're not going to be getting your bits out, are you??'

MUM. That is a very reductive stance to have on a whole spectrum of diverse performance work, which utilises –

'–Don't get snippy, I'm sure some of it is really very good. *I* just don't necessarily *want* to look at someone's bits.'

(Pause.) Fair enough. Look, I know so many amazing artists who work incredibly hard on these projects, publicly engaged, vital, urgent, with Arts Council funding…

An abrupt fade to a soft spotlight, into which HANNAH gazes longingly, letting the wiglet relax, momentarily. The word 'someday' is sung, from 'Somewhere (There's A Place For Us)' in West Side Story.

Return to previous state. The wiglet is re-animated and visibly distressed.

'Are you saying I don't work hard on *my* shows?'

40

No! Mum, I would never disparage one of your shows
– God forbid – I just aspire to something more…
(Wiglet is insulted.) …more *challenging!* I want to craft
something densely layered and resonant to a wide range
of audiences. You know? I don't want to just take a few
nights each year to jump about in front of a bunch of my
family and friends.

*HANNAH and the wiglet slowly turn to face the audience, who
undoubtedly reflect the wide cross-section of society who love to take
a gamble on some fringe performance despite no prior knowledge of
or connect to the Artist.*

… Let's crack on.

Chairs are cleared.

It's always good to dive straight into the second half with a
big number.

*Music plays: the instrumental version of 'Modern Major General'
from* Pirates of Penzance *by Gilbert and Sullivan. HANNAH
potters about the stage in the stilted gait of the Major, her hands
clasped in front of her in a slightly butcher way. She sings some
new lyrics:*

HANNAH: 'I am the very likeness of a learned urban lesbian
My talents tie together both the Sapphic and the thespian
My face is free of make-up and my hair and nails are ever cut
I never wear perfume but my conditioner is coconut
I listen to the music that the heteros have never heard
Were I to wear a skirt then I would strike a picture
quite absurd
My cigarettes are tightly rolled within a Rizla liquorice
*(Mimes holding a cigarette between two fingers, which spread as
they are raised to her mouth.)*
…and I can find my way around most anyone's…
HYPOTENUSE!'

She quickly raises another hand to make a triangle with her fingers.
March-shuffles around the stage again as the Major, towards the
audience as the music reaches the second verse –

– that's as many lyrics as I wrote. It's incredibly hard.
Gilbert and Sullivan were GENIUSES.

The lights go down to soft and gold. Another song begins to play,
the opening notes of 'When London Is Saying Goodnight', sung by
Rita Williams and Billy Thorburn.

HANNAH turns around, produces a small remote control, which she
points at the row of candles upstage, turning them all on one by one.

She walks upstage and raises a new backdrop, of London. It is busy,
dark, vivid, conceptual: Art. She collects up the little candles whilst
singing the first lines along with Rita:

HANNAH moves centre, carrying the candles. She kneels, as Rita
continues singing.

We did this song in the Music Hall once, and it's very
misleading:
the lights don't go down on London.
No matter the smallness of the hour,
the streets remain honey-glazed in gold,
illuminating the activities *(Placing the candles in a ring*
around her on each line.)
of the club-goers
and shift workers
and gangsters
and prostitutes
and, for the last seven years, *(Holding up last candle.)*
me.
I'm near-fluent in London
I know when to walk,
when to run,

42

the choreography of crowds,
step-ball-changing through packed traffic
and hustling commuters.
I know the erotic jolt of pleasure
at seeing a double decker bus after being away for a while
I know the well-rehearsed silence of sitting on the Tube
with strangers
I know all the lines.
And the DLR.

The smoky town is right within my range
and gives me the same tingly feeling as all good harmonies.

She sits back, eyes closed and sings a harmony line in and around Rita's voice.

(Standing up.) One of my best nights in London
was a birthday I had a few years ago.
There were dozens of us.
(Spinning, pointing at each candle.) There was a pub
and another pub
and a club
and a queer night
and a fetish bar
and the colours whirled
and the lights danced
and I'd only taken like half of one.
(As Rita sings the same three words.) As midnight died,
I found myself in this basement
packed with charming, churning, gurning bodies
and through the bright golden haze
came one particular face
I could grow accustomed to.

HANNAH waltzes by herself as the music builds. Eventually an invisible partner seems to spin away from her. She is drunk. She loudly drags the two chairs back together centre stage, flops, curled up on top of them. As each of the final plucks of violin are heard, she clicks off the candles one by one, tucks in and closes her eyes.

Lights fade back slowly, cold.

HANNAH: *(In same position.)* I'm not actually sleeping.

This is acting.

(Sits up.) 'Wakes with start!'

(Grimaces.) 'Urgh, hungover!'

(Hand to head.) 'What's the time??'

(Looks at wrist.) 'Pretend-watch time?! Fuck!'

She hurriedly picks up the candles, dumps them on top of the keyboard. She picks up the suitcase, returns centre stage, produces a single train ticket from her pocket. Waits. She begins to whistle the melody to the verse of 'O, What A Beautiful Morning' from Oklahoma! *On the final line ('an' it looks like it's climbin' right up to the sky'), she slows down the whistle, turning her head as 'carriages' rush past. It slows right down as the train comes to a standstill.*

A beeping sound. The train announcement:

VOICE: 'Doors opening.'

HANNAH steps forward.

Blackout, with blue at back. The TV is blue. ALISON's voice is heard, as HANNAH steps 'onto the train' and sits down – on the SR chair this time.

ALISON: At my very, very first rehearsal I'd ever been to in my life, I was twenty years old, and I walked in the door, and – I was late. And rehearsal was in progress. And I was very shy, cos I was on my own, and I said: 'Is this where the play is?' And this lady, this elderly lady, looks at me,

44

and she said: 'What, dear?' And I said: 'Is this where
the play is?' And she said: 'Well if you mean the *operetta*,
then yes.' And that was your grandmother – Sorry! No it
wasn't! It was your GREAT-grandmother. *(Laughter.)*

*Cold light returns, some from SR. HANNAH's eyeliner is smudged,
her hair is messed, her tie is crooked. A pause.*

HANNAH: *(Tentatively.)* Sometimes, on these journeys,
home can feel further away than it actually is.
Maybe I've just started seeing someone
still so new that even a short distance feels like a wrench.
Maybe the World Cup is on
and all the St George flags beyond the M25 feel a bit…
maybe my team just lost
another election.
Or…
maybe I just accidentally got on the slow train via
New Barnet.

It's probably just the comedown,
but I'm feeling particularly on edge.
Anxious about stepping out onto that platform,
anticipating eyes upon me,
mutterings in the stalls,
the potential for a back-row heckle.
Don't get me wrong
it's a rare and often amusing thing for me to get any shit in
Hertfordshire.
And yet
the closer we get to Welwyn Garden
The more I can feel something stern and forthright
hardening within me.
Wanting me to make sure everyone knows that I'm not
from round here.

45

Anymore. *(Gets up.)*
Wanting me to make a statement.
(Turns to exit.)
Make an entrance.

Exits SL.

Music from Les Miserables *crashes in, from the bit where they raise the barricade. After four bars of this, HANNAH re-enters, now wearing bright, glittery, emerald Doc Martens. She is lit dramatically, casting huge shadows on the wall. She strides across the stage, removes the 'London' backdrop. Mounting the chairs, she waves it, banner-like, as the music finishes with a booming bass chord. Abruptly, the train announcer:*

VOICE: 'Please mind the gap between the train and the platform.'

The lights return to a warm wash. HANNAH climbs down and approaches the keyboard, dragging the backdrop and a chair behind her. She places the chair at the keyboard.

HANNAH: I wait by the station for a while...
until a gold, Audi, soft-top convertible rolls up,
with room for only hypothetical backseat passengers.

She sits at the keyboard.

Inside I find Mum – *(Middle octave flourish.)*
and Peter – *(Low octave flourish.)*
ready to take me to
Nan and Poppa's house – *(High and very low octave flourish, together.)*
– there's a family occasion, and we're having lunch.
So, *here I am, here I am, here I am again.*
We pull out of the station, down to the fountain, *('three coins in the fountain')*

46

take a right, keep the theatre on our left, over the white bridge.

And there they all are.

There's the HEAT WAVE the *Express* promised,
So we're sat out in the garden.
There are Bacardi and Cokes for the ladies, *(High chord.)*
And cans of Fosters for the men, *(Low chord.)*
and Gin and Tonic for me, *(Middle chord, out of key on black notes.)*
because I ordered it once in 2012 and now it's thought of as the only thing I drink.

Poppa has laid on his famous Meat Platter
('filling up the sausages with this and that')
and everyone expresses their surprise and gratitude
that I am still not yet a vegetarian.

Nan and Mum are still laughing in unison *(Clanging high chord.) (Grimacing.)* which is not melding well with my biting hangover.

And everything is still exactly as it has always been.

I'm feeling vaguely…something something…
so I decide to sit back and let the conversation drift by me for a while.

There are trills of different 'voices' in the respective octaves of Nan, Mum, Peter and Poppa. The sporadic chords of Mum and Nan's 'laughter'. HANNAH glances around, tight-lipped as the trills continue. A short snippet of melody starts in one register, and then is repeated in each octave, overlapping in agreement. HANNAH raises a finger, a small objection, and plays a melody in the middle of the keyboard – similar, but with the addition of sharp notes.

The sharp notes become the main section of 'I Giorni' by Ludovico Einaudi. HANNAH begins to play it emphatically, a grin forming. It becomes clear that her hands are incorrectly positioned too far apart, and the music crunches and slows, flat and off-key. She stops playing. She looks up. The lights feel too bright.

Conversation tries to stick to what's going on in rehearsals,
what the next show might be,
but is incessantly interrupted by my parents and grandparents
tripping up in the minefield of offences I now take.
Mainly based on *Guardian* articles I assume everyone has read –
('I don't believe a word of it.') *(Whatever, fine.)*
and my ever-vigilant feminist outrage –
('There is nothing like a dame.') *(That's disgusting.)*

I feel sure that everyone can feel us
snagging on the cracks that have formed.
There's a part of me that wants to stamp on them loudly,
to make sure they're noticed.
But…maybe it doesn't matter that much.
Maybe it's just in my head
and my comedown
and my clinical anxiety – *('cheer up Charlie')*
Fuck! *(Exhausted, exasperated.)*

But to me
they feel like yawning fissures,
that could open up at any moment
and swallow the brand new patio furniture.

She lowers her eyes.

The table needs clearing.
I try to corner my mum and articulate

the complex, internal struggle that I'm going through –
('something has changed within me')
And
she tells me not to be so dramatic.

(Hitting two middle keys next to each other with each trochee:)
SHE tells *ME* not to BE so DRAMATIC.

I'm going to check train times.

HANNAH gets up and heads to the opposite side of the stage. She pauses in the middle of the stage. She takes out the train ticket. As she looks at it, she rises up onto her toes and clicks the heels of her Docs together, twice. She does this again. She goes over to the corner of the stage where the boater is still lying upside down. She drops the ticket in.

Music begins to play, softly. A rhythm of a violin being plucked, with an oboe being played in a high, gliding melody over the top. Dramatic instrumental of 'Bring Him Home' from Les Miserables, *which is usually played in the quiet after the Final Battle, as the barricade turns upon the rotating stage to reveal the fallen ABC students. Enjolras on his red flag. Little Gavroche. Stirring stuff. Meanwhile –*

– the TV plays, soundlessly, the final number from the Welwyn Thalians' 2009 Old Tyme Music Hall; men and women enter from either side of the red-fringed stage, wearing gaudy sequinned shirts and skirts, interlacing, circling, swaying and lunging. Meanwhile –

– HANNAH takes a step back from the boater. She takes out another train ticket from another pocket. She tries to 'throw' it into the hat. If she succeeds, she takes another step back. If she fails, she takes out another ticket from somewhere and tries again. As the video and music plays, she takes out more and more tickets from different pockets and places, throwing as many into the boater as she can, stepping back further and further. As the music reaches a crescendo, more tickets fall from the ceiling. Is this overkill? HANNAH watches

them fall for a moment, chucks a final handful of tickets at the target, grabs the grey tailcoat and top hat, and walks purposefully offstage.

Blackout, soft blue upstage. The TV is showing the 'Ascot Gavotte' scene from the Welwyn Thalians' 2010 production of My Fair Lady. *Everyone is dressed in lavish dress suits, top hats and dresses, all black, white and grey. They hardly move.*

TIM's voice can be heard, chatter in the background:

TIM: And, I like *(Mum's laughter in background.)* the bit behind the stage as well, actually. You know when you're – you know what it's like when you're walking behind the stage in that lovely blue light, and you can hear people onstage – you know what they're doing, because you know what part it is – and it's nice and quiet, and you always meet the same people on the same thing, on the same journey, cos obviously, they're doing the same thing that you're doing, and ah, y'know…it's brilliant really. *(HANNAH's voice: 'I love that bit too, backstage –')* I do! It's – it is, it's something special, so – everybody when you, when you watch the show from the beginning, y'know from the audience, you just assume that when people walk offstage they vaporise into nothing. They don't do anything, they're just not there anymore. And it's not until you realise when you're *in it* that there's just as much enjoyment round the back of the stage, when you're not on the stage, than when you're on the front of it, y'know? Even sometimes, when you're on the front of the stage doing your acting, it's fine, but you can't talk to anybody, can you? *(Laughing.)* Whereas, ah, when you're round the back you can, y'know, have a bit of a laugh, and… I love it, absolutely love it.

TV goes blank, lights come back.

HANNAH enters in tailcoat and gloves, holding the top hat. She walks over to the keyboard and picks up the bunch of flowers. She leans over from the front of the keyboard and plays the two adjacent middle notes from earlier. It turns into 'Chopsticks'.

Big breath. HANNAH slowly paces the stage, better arranging the flowers, dusting the tailcoat, pottering.

HANNAH's mum's voice can be heard:

MUM: So. Hannah, what you've got to remember is that you are madly in love with this woman, you want to give her those flowers and tell her exactly how you feel. So when you're walking about, you're just strolling around and just waiting *determined* to be on that street...until she comes out. When we did it last time, we had these steps going up to the door, and the side of a house –

HANNAH's voice: 'Well, I haven't got steps there, but I could do some, like, some chairs or something?'

Music begins: instrumental version of 'Street Where You Live' from My Fair Lady. *HANNAH places the chairs centre stage again.*

Yeah, chairs will probably work.

So, Freddie came on stage... *(HANNAH goes SL.)*

– stage right. *(HANNAH goes SR.)*

HANNAH 'enters', as a somewhat unsure Freddie, strolling along the front of the stage.

HANNAH: *(Singing the lines in a completely satisfactory tenor:)*

MUM: Face front!

HANNAH does so, with aplomb, feeling like she's several stories high.

MUM: Back the way you came.

HANNAH strolls in the opposite direction, putting hat on, getting into the swing of it a bit more. She looks around, imagining the street, festooned with larks and lilac trees.

MUM: Yeah! Yeah, that's quite nice, that's good!

HANNAH gestures along the 'street' as the second verse comes to an end.

MUM: – Passion!

HANNAH suddenly spins round to face front, singing twice as loudly.

MUM: Ooh – maybe if you went down on one knee!

She does so. She takes off the hat, and sings the next lines more softly, less as Freddie.

MUM: Yessss! And back towards the house!

She gets up, definitely Freddie again, totally not bothered by any imaginary people stopping and staring. She boldly places one foot up on the chairs, jumping up on them with the swelling of the final words.

MUM: Yes! –

She flourishes the bouquet with one hand, the hat with her other, and holds the last note for an impressive amount of time, during which –

MUM: Yes, yes, so what actually might be quite nice is if you actually came down and sat on the steps?

HANNAH: *(Awkwardly gets down and sits on the back of the chairs.)* '–ive!'

Music ends.

MUM: That was great. Good. Can I go home now? *(Laughter, in unison.)*

Houselights come up a little. HANNAH moves to stand centre downstage. She begins to hand out the plastic flowers to different people in the audience.

HANNAH: Can I give you one of these? Throw them back at me, whenever you feel is most appropriate.

Me and Mum have started this new tradition, where she comes down to London for a night and a day and I find something for us to do. So I normally take her to see some art, or some performance, or some Performance Art. As she describes it to her friends: 'Hannah always takes me to something wonderfully odd!'

The most recent time we did this, I met her at Leicester Square station. I was on one side of the street, and I watched her come up the stairs from the Underground. This flash of bright pink coat amongst all the grey-faced Londoners. *(Eyes closed, picturing route.)* We walked down past all the West End theatregoers, over the Millennium Bridge, round the back of Waterloo Station, into this fringe theatre festival that was going on under the arches, in these graffitied caverns of brick.

Inside were droves of twenty-something queers, clustered around a bar that served a hundred different kinds of gin, and about a dozen different performance spaces.

We went to see a solo performance by a female artist. It was quite a small house; maybe only twelve or thirteen people there. Mum had plenty of sympathy for that. We were the only ones in the front row.

The show was great, but about halfway through the tech went down, and it was a very tech-heavy show so the performer had to stop, come out of character, and talk to the audience whist the technicians fixed it.

The performer was really chill about it, which calmed my mother, who had been digging her nails into my leg since it started to go wrong. They chatted with the audience: things like 'anyone got a joke they'd like to share?' or 'anyone got a show they'd like to promote?' Which is quite a common question to ask in the middle of a fringe theatre festival. Most of the audience are people doing shows at other times as part of the programme, you know – 'yeah, we got some spoken word on later tonight' or 'yeah, we got an immersive theatre piece down in the basement.'

But none of those people put their hands up.

The only hand that went up, without any hesitation, was Mum's. In the front row.

The performer was a little taken aback by her enthusiasm, the only person over fifty in the room, still wearing a fuchsia coat.

(As the PERFORMER:) 'Er, sure, go ahead!'

And there was I, sat next to her, thinking, 'Oh, bless her. She's going to promote my show. This one. And that's going to be so odd, because it's not part of this Festival, it's not on any time soon, I'm not sure how much crossover appeal it has with this audience.'

HANNAH smiles and shakes her head, slowly.

(Hand in the air, as MUM:) 'Made In Dagenham!'

(As the PERFORMER, confused:) 'That's a musical right? On the West End? Are you, recommending it?'

(As MUM, rolling her eyes:) 'No no, it's off the West End now. They've released the amateur rights. And I'm doing it. Welwyn Garden City, Hawthorne Theatre, May 9th to 12th.'

Hope you caught it, it was very good.

That's pretty up to date, so that's probably how we have to finish that story. But that's not how you finish a show…

One good way to end a show is how we always ended the Old Tyme Music Hall: no matter the theme or the content of the production, we always, always, ended with this one song from *Chorus Line* – 'She's The One'.

The choreography was always the same. The entire cast would come on, from the two upstage entrances, half through each. As the music started, they would march down and interlace in the middle, to make a 'V'. I would always end up here, and Mum would be right there. And you sway and sway, and lunge and lunge, and on the last bit you would lift your hands up to the centre back of the stage and a curtain would fall and there would be a picture of the Queen.

It's a lot more fun with more people.

HANNAH approaches the audience and pulls people out, naming them:

HANNAH: Can I have Jackie, Gill, Vinny, Terry, Tim, Peter, Alison, Alison and Alison.

HANNAH arranges them into two groups of four and walks them through the Very Simple Choreography. They will enter on either side of the stage, interlace diagonally, form a 'V'. Lunge one way, then the other. Then raise their arms to the middle behind them.

Once they've sort of got it, HANNAH gets them to help clear the stage. They help her put up a slightly tired-looking glitter curtain.

HANNAH asks for the music to begin. It is a recording taken from the 2007 Thalians' Old Tyme Music Hall final number – 'She's The One'.

The stage is lit in various mismatching colours. HANNAH clicks on the candles with the remote, like footlights.

HANNAH stands at the front of the stage, facing back, directing the eight audience members, lunging with them, yelling over the music, singing along where possible.

As their arms swing up to the middle, HANNAH darts in between them, gets them all to hold hands and bow. The audience (hopefully) throws their flowers on the stage before them. On the TV, a black and white photo appears, which may be HANNAH's great-grandmother, or perhaps just the Queen.

End.

Hannah Maxwell & Amanda Sayers in Conversation

HANNAH: What did you think of Brian's foreword?

AMANDA/(MUM): That was lovely. Obviously a man who loves his amdram. If people think of amdram like that then we're not in a bad place, despite the rest of the world going mad. People in the arts often come from that kind of background. You never get rid of it, as much as you try. It's there inside of you.

H: A lot of people are in denial about how formative it might have been.

A: Absolutely – because it's not trendy! Musical amdram is not trendy in the least, but it keeps carrying on. People just love it, you know, they go 'this is the greatest experience of my life!' It probably isn't, but at that time they just find it amazing.

H: I remember. It's a very special feeling being on that stage.

A: Yes, absolutely. When would they have that chance to do that? Live music and the microphones and the set and the big stage and the proper dressing room with the lights... you just feel that you are performing professionally, even though you're not.

H: How important do you think that is to the experience, for it to be close to an idea of a professional performance?

A: I think it's very – are you interviewing me now or are we just chatting?

H: Er, both.

A: Okay. Well I think it's very important, in musicals particularly, that the actors have that kind of experience. It makes it all worthwhile. For them. And certainly for me as well. Because you think it's something special. You can tell that money has been spent on it and people are taking this seriously even if none of them are being paid to do it.

H: Tell me what it was like growing up within the Welwyn Thalians.

A: That's a nice question. For me it was just part of life. Having both your parents heavily involved, and obviously your grandmother being involved as well, it was just –

H: – my great-grandmother?

A: – your great-grandmother, yes. It was just kind of part of life. I do remember occasionally when they couldn't get babysitters I used to be taken to the Hall to watch what was going on. I loved the music. It was so vibrant. Everybody was singing and dancing and I was sitting there tapping my feet to all the tunes just thinking I wanted to be part of it. And of course then I was. *(Laughs.)* My parents would be singing around the house, songs from various musicals that they were in, so it was just always there in the background. It was like having a constant fairy story in your life.

H: Did you ever harbour ambitions about working in theatre professionally?

A: Yes I did. I really wanted to be a professional actress. In fact, I auditioned at the age of fourteen to be part of the National Youth Theatre. Unfortunately I didn't get it. But looking back now, I think I've probably had opportunities to play more parts in the amateur world than I ever would have got being professional. If you think about people in musicals now, they often spend years just doing one part, whereas I got the opportunity to do different parts every year. So for me, I don't know whether actually my life was such a failure really!

H: Can you tell me about a particularly memorable moment in your theatrical life?

A: Okay. I think one of my favourite musicals was *West Side Story*, which I did in my twenties. I got the opportunity to play Anita, which was an amazing part. There was this one scene, where the Jets gang attempted to rape me. They put me on the table and one of the Jets got on top of me, but it was… I could feel the tension amongst them and I physically felt afraid that that was actually going to happen to me. Even though I was onstage and there were loads of people watching. There was the power of the music underneath all this action and I was completely *out,* I forgot that I was Amanda and playing this part. I *was* that part and I was going to be raped at any moment. Some people don't realise that musicals are as strong and profound as plays without music. It's clever musical arrangement that can bring that kind of emotion.

H: I've seen you get really stressed about putting on shows, especially when it's getting close to show week when things aren't quite ready. What is it about the experience that makes you want to put yourself through this for no money?

A: I think for me it's seeing my imagination come to life. I think that's it. When I've got my script and my score and my notepad and I'm writing down where everyone's standing, where they're moving to and little arrows and everything, and I've gone prancing around the kitchen, listening to the music and trying to get it to work in my head, and then I go out with this huge group of people, with a myriad of differing abilities – and it works!

They're enjoying it, I'm liking it and it's just an incredible experience when it works. Especially when people come up to you and say, 'I really enjoyed that, thank you.'

H: When I was younger, I remember conversations with you and Nan along the lines of, 'Oh, the next time that we do whatever show, you'll be able to be that part,' looking at me. Did you assume that I would take up the Thalians mantle, and at what point did your mind maybe change about that?

A: Well, you were always a very serious actor. I'm not sure I ever thought... I thought you'd be very particular about the parts that you wanted to play because I always thought you took yourself quite seriously. And in musicals you can't take yourself seriously. There was always... I'm not sure 'bemusement' is the word...but I made you do a lot of things that you weren't comfortable with. I remember in...what was the show in 2009 where I got you to do the can-can?

H: *Calamity Jane.*

A: *Calamity Jane! (Laughs.)* And it was that bizarreness... You certainly weren't comfortable being a dancer. I think you quite liked singing. I could see at twelve that you were good, but you were also very lazy in terms of what you wanted to do at that stage. It's only as you got older that you seemed interested. Certainly when you auditioned for Eliza, funnily enough – I know you put that into your show – you were actually really good as Eliza! And I think that surprised me. I knew you were a good actress, but I didn't realise you could sing as well as you could. So, well done you. *(Laughs.)*

H: It's strange, but that really means a lot to me even now.

A: What, that I thought you were good?

H: Yeah. It's such a world away, but it means a lot to hear you say that you thought I was a good potential Eliza. Obviously, now I've wandered off into various non-conventional directions...

A: But that adds colour to everything though, doesn't it?

H: Indeed it does. I've taken you to some alternative performance things, some Live Art. What did you think about coming to those different kinds of shows?

A: I loved the Sh!t Theatre and the Split Britches. Oh yeah, and the holding hands thing that you took my on as well.

H: *Walking: Holding*?[1]

A: Yeah! Funnily enough, I enjoyed that just because you were there. Because you said it was alright and you'd be hiding behind lampposts to make sure I was okay. I found it a very liberating experience.

H: Rosana said you made quite an impression on the performers.

A: Did I?

H: I think most people who sign up for those kinds of experiences at performance festivals have a mindset more similar to that of a visitor to an art gallery. Most people just walk along quietly and think about the significance of being seen to hold hands with different kinds of bodies in public. You were very much in 'I'm on my holiday' mode –

---

1 *Walking: Holding* is an experimental performance by artist Rosana Cade, where one audience members walks along a carefully designed route around a city (in Mum's case, Berlin), holding hands with a range of different people.

A: – I chatted to them all! Oh, I'm sorry. Part of my
nervousness, that is – but also I was genuinely interested
in why they would be doing this. And if I've got to hold
hands with people I've got to talk to them. I didn't realise
I was an oddity in that respect. I'll be quiet next time.

H: Not at all, please! A lot of my show is about the feeling of
coming back to your hometown after you've left. Would
you be able to tell me about a difficult period in our
relationship since I moved out of home?

A: Hmm. I find you very interesting. I'm not sure I find you
difficult. I mean, bless you, you come and see everything
that I do, when you can, and we always have interesting
discussions afterwards. It's always aspects of the shows
that I never quite think about. Maybe I berate myself a
little that I look at it as written rather than think about
how it is perceived today. But whether that's an issue
between you and me, I don't know. I mean you've never
been unsupportive of what I do and you always come
along with great interest. You never belittle it, which
is what I like, but you also present me with interesting
opposing considerations that I hadn't thought about.
Is that a right way of putting it? In many ways I think
I've got closer to you since you moved away than I was
when you were here. You certainly open my eyes to a
different view than I would have thought before and I'm
not sure that's necessarily a bad thing.

H: What were your thoughts or feelings when you saw the
show for the first time?

A: I actually was very nervous about going to see it. I
suppose a little of me was concerned about how much
piss-taking there was going to be, and if I was going to
have to take it on the chin. I didn't want to see everything
I'd done, everything the family had done, completely

trashed – just because it was an easy thing to do, but you didn't do that. I liked the take you did on it, interspersed with your own feelings of growing up and coming out and your sexuality. You could have hardened it a lot more. But I thought what you did was really beautiful, even the slight criticisms of what we did or how we did them was done in a very warm way. I was very proud of you for doing that. Because you must have had to be quite careful, especially when you knew that members of the family where going to be there.

H: I was certainly very nervous when you came the first time. I remember I came out after and I couldn't find you.

A: Yes, you rang me because you thought I'd taken offence and stormed off. I only went over to the pub so I could get you a pint in, because the Camden Theatre was so crowded. *(Laughs.)*

H: Would you ever want to make something autobiographical like that, yourself?

A: Funnily enough, yes, if I didn't think I was being self-indulgent.

H: It's always a danger.

A: If I thought anybody would be interested in my story, but… Watching what you've made has actually got me thinking that what I've done over the years has been quite interesting… I'll probably never do it, but yes, I think if I'm honest, I would love to write something about my experience growing up in that world, going out from the 70s to now.

H: What do you want to achieve in your theatrical life before you hang up your ringbinder?

A: I would like there to be some people who want to take on the mantle of directing shows for the Thalians and love it for what it is and keep it going for the future. I would ultimately like to expand the people in the Thalians so that I leave it with more people than there was when I started. But most importantly I want to promote the love of this art. I'd love that legacy to continue, to get more people off their Xbox, to go out there and want to perform in front of people, and want to sing and want to do something that's good for the soul rather than just good for their fingers. I think that would be a great epitaph for me.

H: It's important, then. Amateur dramatics.

A: Well it's been important for me. I don't want to foist it on the world but I would hate to see it just die. Hopefully, if it wasn't for what I've done, you wouldn't be doing this either. So if you can bring that kind of love to this kind of art, then I can ask for no more.

H: We've been talking for an hour! This is going to take a lot of editing.

A: How did I do? Was that alright? It came from the heart. I mean, I didn't think about it, it just came out of my mouth. It shows that my enthusiasm for it has not waned, at least. *(Laughs.)*